D1524815

EXTREME SNOW VEHICLES

IAN F. MAHANEY

PowerKiDS press

New York

Published in 2016 by
The Rosen Publishing Group, Inc.
29 East 21st Street, New York, NY 10010

Developed and produced for Rosen by BlueAppleWorks Inc.

Art Director: T. J. Choleva
Managing Editor for BlueAppleWorks: Melissa McClellan
Designer: Joshua Avramson
Photo Research: Jane Reid
Editor: Marcia Abramson

Photo Credits:
Cover Fotokvadrat/Shutterstock; title page Fedor Korolevskiy/Shutterstock; p. 4 left Serjio74/Shutterstock; p. 4–5 vichie81/Shutterstock; p. 5 right US Mission Canada/Creative Commons; p. 6 left Marco Barone/Shutterstock; p. 6–7 Maxim Petrichuk/Shutterstock; p. 7 top Jaroslav Moravcik/Shutterstock; p. 8–9 Sergei Butorin/Shutterstock; p. 9 left onixxino/Shutterstock; p. 9 right Sinisa Botas/Shutterstock; p. 10 Tyler Olson/Shutterstock; p. 10 top Jerry Zitterman/Shutterstock; p. 10–11 Volodymyr Burdiak/Shutterstock; p. 11 top Mindscape studio/Shutterstock; p. 12 Aleksei Lazukov/Shutterstock; p. 12–13 glen gaffney/Shutterstock; p. 13 bottom Sergei Butorin/Shutterstock; p. 13 top Art Konovalov/Shutterstock; p. 14–15 steve estvanik/Shutterstock; p. 15 right Benoit Daoust/Shutterstock; p. 16 bottom, 16–17, 17 right Kabelleger/David Gubler/Creative Commons; p. 16 top Anton Romanov/Dreamstime; p. 17 top antb/Shutterstock; p. 18 MTA Long Island Rail Road/Creative Commons; p. 18–19 JoSchmaltz/Creative Commons; p. 19 top Steve Collender/Shutterstock; p. 20 left Jim West/ Keystone Press; p. 20–21 Philip Bird LRPS CPAGB/Shutterstock; p. 21 top Timothy Smith - Tas50/Creative Commons; p. 22 John Lloyd/Creative Commons; p. 23 left, 23 top Melensdad/Creative Commons; p. 23 right courtesy of Track-N-Go; p. 24 Frontiersnorth/Creative Commons; p. 24–25 Carlyn Iverson; p. 25 top Eli Duke/Creative Commons; p. 26 left Franke 1/Creative Commons; p. 26–27, 27 top POA(Phot) Mez Merrill/MOD/Open Government Licence; p. 28 Lars Magne Hovtun/Norwegian Armed Forces; p. 28 top Audun Braastad/Norwegian Armed Forces; p. 28–29 Torbjørn Kjosvold/Norweigan Armed Forces.

Cataloging-in-Publication-Data
Mahaney, Ian F.
Extreme snow vehicles / by Ian F. Mahaney.
p. cm. — (Extreme machines)
Includes index.
ISBN 978-1-4994-1187-4 (pbk.)
ISBN 978-1-4994-1215-4 (6 pack)
ISBN 978-1-4994-1216-1 (library binding)
1. Snowmobiles — Juvenile literature. 2. Snow removal — Juvenile literature.
3. Snowplows — Juvenile literature. I. Mahaney, Ian F. II. Title.
TD868.M3484 2016
629.225—d23

Manufactured in the United States of America
CPSIA Compliance Information: Batch #WS15PK: For Further Information contact: Rosen Publishing, New York, New York at 1-800-237-9932

Contents

What Are Snow Vehicles? 4

SLOPES AND TRAILS

Mighty Snowcats 6

Snow Cannons 8

Fast Snowmobiles 10

Extreme Snow Races 12

SNOW-FIGHTING MACHINES

Snow Busters 14

Awesome Railway Plows 16

Extreme Snow Melting 18

FAR-OFF PLACES

Snow-Going Buses 20

Extreme Snow Cars 22

Exploring the Poles 24

IN THE MILITARY

Extreme Snow Transporters 26

Mobile Snow Warriors 28

GLOSSARY 30

FOR MORE INFORMATION 31

INDEX 32

What Are Snow Vehicles?

Snow vehicles are powerful extreme machines used to drive in snowy and icy conditions. Inventors, engineers, and **entrepreneurs** have made vehicles that can handle extreme weather. These machines can take people to some of the coldest places on earth. Soon enough, there may be extreme machines that can help people accomplish even more work in snowy **environments**. These machines could help people have more fun during winter, too.

The Bombardier B12 was an early model of snow bus that could hold 12 people. It is an ancestor of today's snow coaches.

Work and Fun

Extreme snow machines help us do a lot of work or have a lot of fun. These powerful vehicles can help us remove snow from parking lots or drive to the coldest places on Earth. We can ride to the tops of snowy mountains in **gondolas** or other big vehicles. We can drive on snow or frozen lakes faster than we can ski or skate. This book will explore extreme snow machines and how people use them to work and play.

The modern snowmobile was developed from the snow coach by Canadian inventor Joseph-Armand Bombardier.

Snow coaches are built on tracks that help them carry passengers and parcels over snow and ice.

Mighty Snowcats

Driving in the winter is hard. Cars slip on ice. They also sink in deep snow. There are extreme vehicles for riding in the snow, though. Many of these vehicles have huge tires for gripping snow and ice. Other extreme vehicles have continuous tracks. They are designed to maintain traction and stay on top of soft and wet surfaces. Tanks and bulldozers are examples of mighty continuous track vehicles.

Snowcats are huge continuous track vehicles that are made to travel on snow. Snowcats either have two or four tracks. The tracks are made of rubber, steel, or other metal, and the driver of a snowcat can control the movement of each track.

This snowcat uses wide rubber tracks with steel attachments to gain traction and stay on top of snow.

Ski resorts use snowcats to groom their slopes by smoothing out the snow. Other types of snowcats are used to carry passengers up and down snow-covered mountains.

A trail groomer is another name for the special type of snowcat used to smooth out ski and snowmobile trails.

Wide Snow Busters

Snowcats have tracks that can be as big as five feet (1.5 m) wide. Those enormous tracks distribute a snowcat's weight so it does not sink in deep snow. Snowcats also have controls that let the vehicle ride over rough **terrain**. These tracks grab hold of the snow, and let the snowcat climb hills and mountains where no other large vehicles can go.

Snow Cannons

To make snow, freezing water and pressurized air are shot through machines called snow guns or cannons.

Ski resorts use snowcats and other snow vehicles to transport skiers and to keep skiing slopes in good shape. Ski resort operators have to make sure that the level of snow on slopes is just right. If there is too much snow, they groom the slopes with snowcats. If there is not enough, they use snow machines to add some. These machines are called snowmakers.

Did You Know?

Workers at the 2014 Winter Olympics in Sochi, Russia, used 550 snow cannons to make snow for the ski and snowboarding events.

Snowmaking was invented in 1950 in New York. Now the machines come in many shapes and sizes.

Powerful Snow Blasters

To snow, the temperature in the **atmosphere** must be lower than 32° Fahrenheit (0° Celsius). There must also be moisture in the clouds. Without these two conditions, it will not snow. If it is cold enough to snow, but there is not enough moisture in the air, an extreme snow machine can make snow. Snowmaking machines work by shooting freezing water into air that is cold enough so that snow crystals form.

Snowmakers are powerful today. In fact, big snowmakers are called snow cannons. Most ski areas around the world have snowmaking equipment so they can make snow when natural conditions aren't right for it to snow. Snow cannons today can shoot water and snow more than 30 feet (9 m) into the air. The freezing water is shot so high in the air so that the water has time to further freeze on its way down to the ground. Big snow cannons can make snow 12 inches (30 cm) deep that covers more than two **acres** in about 12 hours.

Fast Snowmobiles

Snowmobiles are extreme snow machines. They are much smaller than snowcats. Most snowmobiles are designed for only one rider besides the driver.

Snowmobiles can reach top speeds in open areas such as frozen lakes. Snowmobile riders also like to ride on trails, climb mountains, and compete in snowmobile races.

Snowmobiles have powerful engines that drive a continuous track. The continuous track on the back of snowmobiles is normally made of Kevlar. Kevlar is a **synthetic** material that is stronger and lighter than steel. Snowmobiles also have skis on the front of the sleds. Handlebars allow the driver to control the skis and direction of the snowmobile.

Snowmobiles have skis in front and a track in back. They are fuel-efficient and have replaced dogsleds in many areas as the best way to transport people and small loads.

Snowmobiles have small and lightweight engines, but they are very fast. Specialized snowmobiles have been clocked going more than 190 miles (306 km) per hour on land and 170 miles (274 km) per hour over frozen water.

Snowmobiles help people in remote areas get together, run errands, and enjoy the outdoors.

It takes skill, strength, and good reflexes to drive a high-speed snowmobile over slick snow.

Faster Than All

Many companies make fast snowmobiles. One of the fastest snowmobiles is made by the Arctic Cat company. It is the XF1100 Turbo Sno Pro and can go faster than 100 miles (161 km) per hour. The XF1100 Turbo can travel on snowmobile trails as well as up mountainsides for great views and tours of the wilderness.

Extreme Snow Races

Snowmobile racing is a popular sport in Canada and northern parts of the United States. Snocross is a sport where snowmobile riders race around a course with tight turns, hills, and jumps. The longest snowmobile race in the world is held every year in Alaska. The race is 2,031 miles (3,268 km) long and called the Iron Dog.

One of the largest snowmobile races in the world is the International 500. It is 500 miles (805 km) long and has been run in Michigan since 1968. Riders from Canada and the United States compete every year to be its champion.

In snowmobile racing, riders race on snowmobiles that are not available for sale. The manufacturers make **custom** models for the racers. The manufacturers **sponsor** these events and try to sell similar snowmobile models to the racing fans.

When there is no snow, snowmobiles still compete on grass or asphalt in drag races. One of the biggest drag races, called Hay Days, is held in Minnesota.

Races on Grass and Water

One form of racing is drag racing. **Competitors** race 500 feet (152 m) on their snowmobiles and can reach speeds of 130 miles (209 km) per hour. Snowmobile drag races aren't always held on snow. Sometimes drag races are held on ice, grass, or pavement.

Snowmobilers also race on water. This sport is called snowmobile skipping. Riders drive on water much like water-skiing.

Snowmobiles can even race on water by going very fast and using their wide tracks to stay afloat. Not all areas allow this sport because it can be dangerous.

The Snocross racing series are snowmobile races on a motocross-like course. The races are held during the winter season in the Northern United States and Canada.

Snow-Fighting Machines

Snow Busters

A snowplow truck uses an attached blade to push snow out of the way. Snowplows can be huge or small.

A snowplow is a machine attached to the front of a truck. A plow is more **efficient** at clearing snow than a shovel.

In snowy areas, many people turn pickup trucks into snowplows by attaching a blade under the front bumper. Pickups clear driveways, small parking lots, and sometimes residential streets by pushing the snowplow blade. Depending on the size of the job, these plows either push snow forward or the driver angles the blade so the plow pushes the snow to the side of the road. These snowplows are normally six feet (1.8 m) to eight feet (2.4 m) wide, and two feet (0.6 m) to three feet (0.9 m) tall.

Clearing Airport Runways

Clearing snow from an airport's runway is important in winter. The plows that clear runways are huge. Sometimes plows with a straight blade clear the runway. Other times, big rotary plows clear the path for the planes.

In big snowstorms, tandem plows work together to clear major highways quickly.

Getting the Job Done

For bigger jobs, bigger plows clear the roads. Dump trucks often have plows attached to their front end. These plows look like larger versions of pickup plows and these big plows push snow to the side of the road. Other big plows are shaped like the letter V. These plows push snow to both sides of the road. Still other big haulers are called rotary plows. These plows blow snow far from the road.

Tandem plows work together. The first plow clears the road and the second plow clears any snow the first plow missed.

Awesome Railway Plows

Railroad service is important in the United States and around the world. Snow can stop the trains, though, almost as easily as snow can stop a car. It's also dangerous for trains to travel on icy or snow-covered tracks. Extreme snow machines can clear the tracks of snow so trains can pass.

Train companies use powerful locomotives **equipped** with plows to clear the way. Often, V-shaped plows as tall as the locomotives stand in front of these powerful snow-clearing trains. These trains with V-shaped plows clear the tracks just as snowplows clear the highways. The trains push snow to either side of the tracks.

Many locomotives use a V-shaped plow. The snow slides over the plow and falls away to the side of the tracks.

Instead of a plow, giant snowblowers sometimes are attached to the front of a locomotive.

Railroads need a more extreme machine to clear really deep snow. Rotary plows like this one chop up all the snow in their path.

Tunnel Diggers

When the snow is too deep for even the massive V-shaped plows, railroad companies have a better, more powerful plow they can use. Deep snow often covers train tracks in the Rocky Mountains. When it does, railway companies can use a rotary snowplow to clear the way. These rotary plows look like giant fans at the front of the train. Rotary plows chop up snow and shoot it to either the left or right of the train tracks. Rotary blades are extreme. They can clear snow that is 20 feet (6.1 meters) deep.

Extreme Snow Melting

The purpose of clearing snow is to make sidewalks, streets, and train tracks safe to use. Sometimes it helps to melt the snow and ice while clearing it.

Many trucks with snowplows have spreaders at the back end. The spreader drops salt to melt snow. The spreader can also drop sand to improve vehicles' grip of the road. Sometimes, building owners install heating cables or coils under a roof or driveway to melt snow and ice.

Extreme snow machines are also needed to melt more snow and ice. Railroads use deicing cars to keep tracks and especially the third rail free of ice. The third rail is the rail that powers electric trains with electricity.

Jet blowers use blasts of hot air from their **turbine engine** to melt ice and snow and then blow it away from the railway tracks.

A box snowplow scoops up snow and takes it to a machine that melts it. The snow turns into water and flows into drains or sewers.

It takes many snow melters to clear runways at big airports such as John F. Kennedy Airport in New York.

Heavy-Duty Melting

When there's too much snow in a parking lot, box snowplows can come help clear it. Box snowplows look like small tractors or bulldozers, and pick up snow in a scoop. Then the box plow can haul the snow to a machine that looks like a dump truck or shipping container. The machine is a snow melter that constantly boils water. When the box snowplow drops a scoop of snow in the snow melter, the snow instantly melts and the machine gets rid of the melted snow.

Snow-Going Buses

Special tracks and skis are attached to sight-seeing snow vehicles so tours can be held during the winter at Yellowstone National Park in Wyoming.

Do you think a bus can drive up Mount Washington in New Hampshire or into Yellowstone National Park during the winter? What if it were snowing and a foot of snow sat on the ground? Special buses called snow coaches can. Snow coaches are **modified** to handle deep snow. A mechanic takes the tires off these buses and replaces the tires with four continuous tracks. These buses look like buses, but drive like snowcats. They can go just about anywhere. On other snow coaches, mechanics swap the back wheels for continuous tracks and the front wheels for skis. They are a combination of a bus and a snowmobile. These buses take passengers on tours of places people have trouble visiting on their own.

Researchers at McMurdo Station in Antarctica get around in a modified Terra Bus.

A fleet of 22 Terra Buses takes visitors around Canada's Columbia Icefield and Jasper National Park.

Mighty Terra Buses

Terra Buses are big snow coaches made by a company in Alberta, Canada. Some Terra Buses carry 56 passengers. Other Terra buses are outfitted with scientific equipment to study cold environments in places such as Antarctica. Terra Buses do not have continuous tracks like most snow coaches. Terra Buses have low-pressure tires instead. Low-pressure tires increase the area that the tires touch on the ground. This increases the bus's traction and helps it handle snow and ice.

Extreme Snow Cars

Cars have become stuck in the snow ever since cars were invented. Tires sink in the snow, and many entrepreneurs over the years have tried to figure out solutions to fix the problem. Big grooved tires help traction in the snow. Like the Terra Bus, reducing tire pressure in a car increases the contact that tires have with the ground.

Some entrepreneurs have even invented better cars for the snow. Before snowmobiles and snowcats, entrepreneurs tried to make cars with skis and tracked tires. An entrepreneur put skis and a propeller on the back of another car. Someone affixed skis and tracks to the Model T, a famous early car made by Henry Ford.

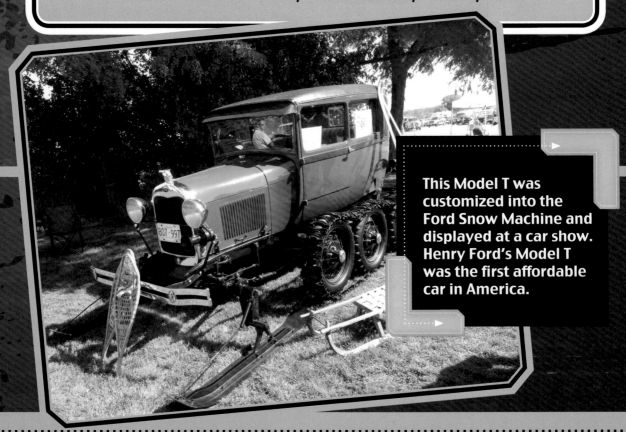

This Model T was customized into the Ford Snow Machine and displayed at a car show. Henry Ford's Model T was the first affordable car in America.

Made for the Snow

One extreme vehicle was called the Snow Trac. It was made from 1957 to 1980 and was about 12 feet (3.7 m) long and 6 feet (1.8 m) wide. This is about the size of a small modern car. Snow Tracs could fit seven passengers and looked like small ice cream trucks on tractor tracks.

There are companies that specialize in producing triangular-tracked systems that can be installed on regular cars to give them the ability to drive in deep snow. It usually requires removing the wheels and replacing them with temporary tracks.

Track-N-Go

A new Canadian company makes a track system call Track-N-Go. Four tracks fit under the regular wheels of a pickup truck and allow the pickup to drive like a snowcat through massive snowdrifts.

Snow Tracs still are used for search and rescue, including these vehicles in Iceland.

Exploring the Poles

The North and South Poles are among the coldest places on Earth. Ice fills the seas at the North Pole. The ice is between 6 feet (1.8 m) and 10 feet (3 m) thick. At the South Pole, Antarctica is almost entirely made of ice. The ice on Antarctica measures about 7.5 million square miles (19.5 million square kilometers). That's almost twice the area of all 50 United States.

To explore these remote and cold places, people need extreme vehicles. One such vehicle is the **Tundra** Buggy. It takes people on tours to see polar bears in northern Canada. The Tundra Buggy has massive tires five and a half feet (1.7 m) tall. These tires keep passengers away from the bears. The tires also have huge treads that grip the ice and handle snowdrifts up to 6 feet (1.8 m) tall.

Visitors travel the Arctic on a Tundra Buggy tour. This extreme vehicle has giant tires that grip the ice. They also keep polar bears at a safe distance!

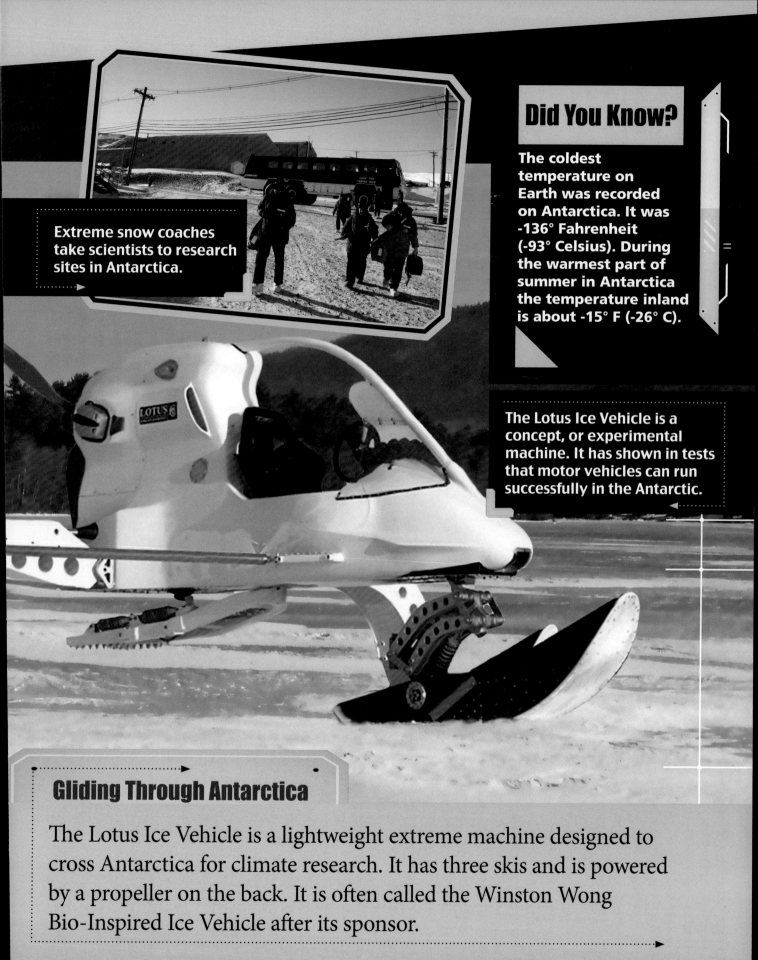

Extreme snow coaches take scientists to research sites in Antarctica.

The Lotus Ice Vehicle is a concept, or experimental machine. It has shown in tests that motor vehicles can run successfully in the Antarctic.

Gliding Through Antarctica

The Lotus Ice Vehicle is a lightweight extreme machine designed to cross Antarctica for climate research. It has three skis and is powered by a propeller on the back. It is often called the Winston Wong Bio-Inspired Ice Vehicle after its sponsor.

In the Military

Extreme Snow Transporters

Soviet forces use an MT-LB troop carrier for winter training.

Military engineers design extreme vehicles that enable soldiers to survive, operate, and fight in extremly cold environments. Some of the best extreme snow vehicles were designed in Finland, Russia, and Sweden. Versions of these vehicles are used by armies of several different countries.

The former Soviet Union's army manufactured a specific kind of tank that is especially good at driving in snow. The MT-LB has extra-wide tracks that allow the tank to grip the slippery earth when covered with ice and snow. Present MT-LB versions are being used by armies around the world.

The Bandvagn can take troops to areas that usually can be reached only by plane or helicopter.

Made-in-Sweden Troop Carriers

Sweden made an even more spacious continuous-tracked vehicle beginning in 1974. The Bandvagn has carried troops from the United States, Canada, and European and Asian countries. It looks like a locomotive with a caboose and can hold 17 people. In addition to military uses, countries such as Iceland have used the Bandvagn to conduct search and rescue missions when civilians are lost in remote locations.

Mobile Snow Warriors

Military operations in severely cold weather are difficult. Soldiers need to undergo special training in how to conduct combat operations and use extreme military snow vehicles in cold weather conditions. In 2014, 16,000 soldiers from 16 nations came to Norway to take part in the exercise Cold Response 2014. Norway is ideally suited for winter activities. The environment there is one of vast amounts of snow, icy weather, and low temperatures.

Participating soldiers did their training in extreme Arctic weather. Heavy snowfall, low temperatures, and blizzard conditions made the exercise especially challenging for the soldiers and their snow vehicles.

The United States, Canada, and 14 European nations sent troops to Norway for winter training in March 2014.

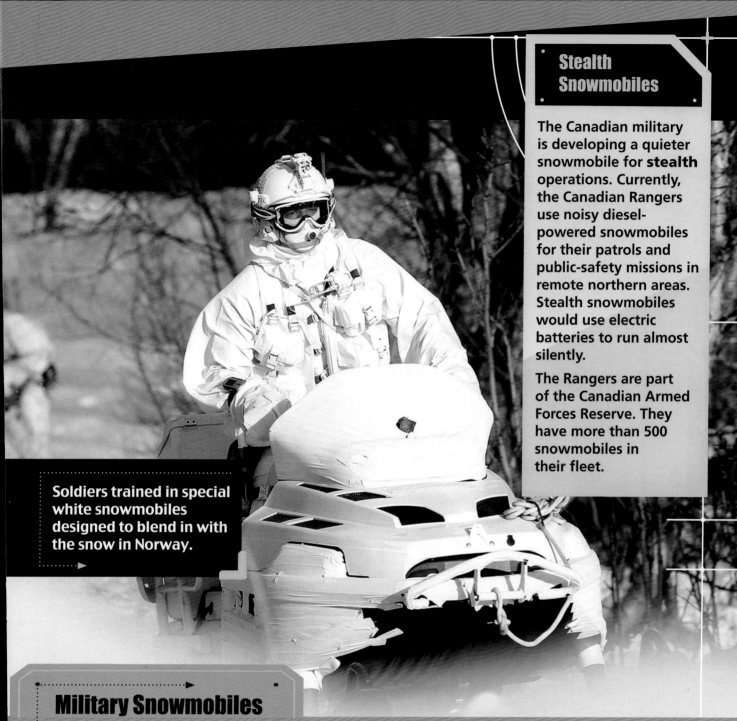

The Canadian military is developing a quieter snowmobile for **stealth** operations. Currently, the Canadian Rangers use noisy diesel-powered snowmobiles for their patrols and public-safety missions in remote northern areas. Stealth snowmobiles would use electric batteries to run almost silently.

The Rangers are part of the Canadian Armed Forces Reserve. They have more than 500 snowmobiles in their fleet.

Soldiers trained in special white snowmobiles designed to blend in with the snow in Norway.

Military Snowmobiles

Military personnel use snowmobiles for **humanitarian** and security purposes. Countries near the Arctic Circle such as the United States, Canada, Norway, and Russia use snowmobiles. Snowmobile troops protect their country's borders, help in search and rescue operations, and conduct **surveillance** for national security. The Cold Response exercise and others like it help train for emergency and wartime situations in extreme winter conditions, and strengthen cooperation between allied countries.

GLOSSARY

acre Units of measure. One acre equals 43,560 square feet (4,047 sq m). If an acre is shaped like a square, an acre is about 209 feet (64 m) on each side.

atmosphere The air above Earth.

competitor Someone who is trying to win or do better than others, especially in sports or business.

custom Something made special for a person.

efficient Done in the quickest, best way possible.

entrepreneurs Businesspeople who have started their own businesses.

environment The surroundings or conditions in which a person, animal, or plant lives or operates.

equipped To be supplied with.

gondolas Vehicles suspended from cables that carry passengers up and down mountains.

humanitarian To care for people and help them.

modified Changed.

sponsor To support the cost of an event.

stealth Secret, sneaky movements.

surveillance Watching what the enemy is doing.

synthetic Something that is not made in nature. It is made by humans.

terrain A piece of land or the physical qualities of a piece of land.

tundra A large area of flat land in northern parts of the world where there are no trees and the ground is always frozen.

turbine engine An engine that converts energy of a moving fluid or gas (water, steam, or air) into mechanical energy.

Further Reading

Friedman, Mel. *Antarctica.*
New York, NY: Scholastic, 2009.

Labrecque, Ellen. *Arctic Tundra.*
Mankato, MN: Raintree, 2013.

Maynard, Christopher. *DK Readers L4: Extreme Machines.*
New York, NY: DK Publishing, 2012.

Older, Jules. *Snowmobile: Bombardier's Dream Machine.*
Watertown, MA: Charlesbridge, 2012.

Von Finn, Denny. *Snowmobiles.*
Minneapolis, MN: Bellwether Media, 2010.

Woods, Bob. *Snowmobile Racers.*
New York, NY: Enslow Publishers, 2010.

Websites

Due to the changing nature of Internet links, PowerKids Press has developed an online list of websites related to the subject of this book. This site is updated regularly. Please use this link to access the list: **www.powerkidslinks.com/em/snow**

INDEX

A

Antarctica 21, 24, 25

atmosphere 9

B

Bandvagn 27

Bombardier B12 4

Bombardier, Joseph-Armand 5

box snowplow 19

C

Cold Response 2014 28

continuous track vehicles 6

D

drag racing 13

E

extreme weather 4

G

gondolas 5

K

Kevlar 10

L

Lotus Ice Vehicle 25

N

North Pole 24

S

ski resorts 7

skis 10, 20, 22, 25

snocross racing 13

snow blasters 9

snow cannons 8, 9

snow coaches 4, 5, 20, 21, 25

Snow Trac 23

snowblowers 17

snowcats 6, 7, 8, 10, 20, 22

snowmobile(s) 5, 7, 10, 11, 12, 13, 20, 29

snowmobile race 12

snowplow 14, 17, 19

South Pole 24

T

Terra Buses 21

trail groomer 7

Tundra Buggy 24

V

v-shaped plow 16

W

winter 4, 6, 9, 13, 15, 20, 26, 28, 29